THE PURPLE COW

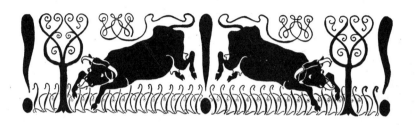

AND OTHER NONSENSE

5Y

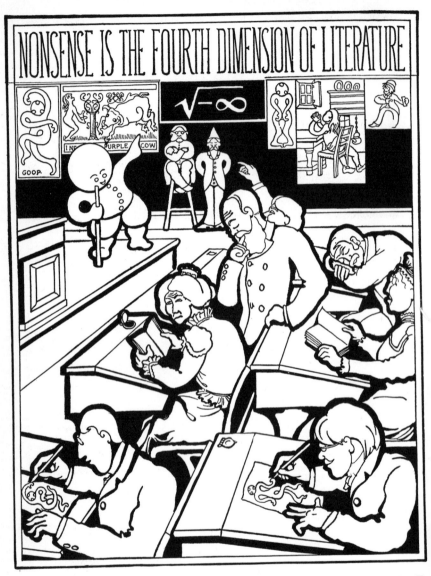

THE NONSENSE SCHOOL

THE PURPLE COW
AND OTHER NONSENSE

Being a Collection of the Humorous Masterpieces of
GELETT BURGESS, ESQ.,
Sometime Editor of the " *Lark*," "*Le Petit Journal des Refusées*," & " *Enfant Terrible* "

With Thirty Odd *Nonsense Quatrains*, BAD *Ballads*,
Poems of PATAGONIA, Curious *Cartoons*,
Autobiographies of Famous GOOPS, & a
Myriad *Impossibilities,* adorned with less than

A Million Heart-Rending Illustrations by the Author

¶ The *Whole* forming a *Book* of Blissful *Bosh* for the *Blasé* ; an
Amusing *Antidote* to Modern *Neurasthenia ;* a Stimulating *Spur*
to *Thoughtlessness, &* a Restful *Recreation* for the *Super-Civilized*,
the *Over-Educated, &* the *Hyper-Refined*.   Carefully Expurgated
of all *Reason, Purpose, & Verisimilitude* by a *Corps* of Irresponsi-
ble *Idiots*.   An Extrageneous *Tome* of *Twaddle*, an Infallible

CYCLOPÆDIA *of* BALDERDASH
Ferocious Fancies & Inconsequential Vagaries
Than which, Nothing could be More So

DOVER PUBLICATIONS, INC.
NEW YORK

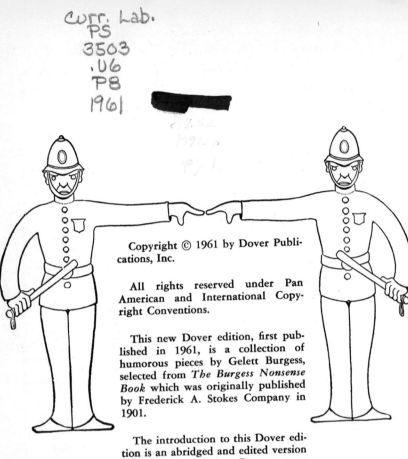

This new Dover edition, first published in 1961, is a collection of humorous pieces by Gelett Burgess, selected from *The Burgess Nonsense Book* which was originally published by Frederick A. Stokes Company in 1901.

The introduction to this Dover edition is an abridged and edited version of the essay, "Gelett Burgess as a Humorist," written by Burgess and included in *Our American Humorists,* edited by Thomas L. Masson and published by Dodd, Mead and Company in 1922.

Manufactured in the United States of America

Dover Publications, Inc.
180 Varick Street
New York 14, N. Y.

*T*O him who vainly conjures sleep
   In counting visionary sheep;
To her who, in the dentist's power
Would fain recall a gayer hour;
To him who visits tiresome aunts,
And comes upon this book by chance;
To her who in the hammock lies,
And, bored with Ibsen, BURGESS tries;
To those who can't remember dates
While nonsense rhymes stick in their pates;
To those who buy, and do not borrow,
Nor put it off until to-morrow;
To all who in these pages look,
I dedicate this Nonsense Book!

Gelett Burgess

PUBLISHER'S NOTE

For an author as widely quoted as the creator of the Purple Cow, Gelett Burgess' work has been paradoxically unavailable in recent years. Everyone knows "I'd rather have fingers than toes" and uses such Burgess coinages as "blurb" and "bromide," while his Purple Cow is forever fixed in the book of American mythological animals. Yet almost none of his writing for adults is now in print, and even in secondhand bookstores his work is hard to come by. People who own Burgess books do not readily give them up.

Gelett Burgess was born in Boston in 1866 and died in 1951. There is much that we might have written about him, but in keeping with the spirit of the book, which is unadulterated Burgess, we have decided to present his own account of his life and have reprinted as an introduction an extract from "Gelett Burgess as a Humorist," by Gelett Burgess, from Thomas L. Masson's *Our American Humorists,* originally published by Dodd, Mead and Company in 1922. The footnotes are our own.

Burgess was one of the most original humorists that America has produced, and this collection, which is a selection from *The Burgess Nonsense Book* originally published by Frederick A. Stokes Company in 1901, contains many of his most unique and truly awe-inspiring pieces. We hope they will provide as much fun and merriment today as they have in the past and that they will help to restore Gelett Burgess to his rightful place in the gallery of American humorists.

The Editors

GELETT BURGESS AS A HUMORIST

by

GELETT BURGESS

If you will clamber up almost any one of the many, many church steeples in Boston—from the New Old South to the Church-of-the-Holy-Beanblowers—you will find, near the top, a curious mark—a monogram composed of the Phoenician letters F. G. B. But Gelett Burgess, in those kidloid days, was really no Steeple Jack. His marks were scrawled inside, not outside those steeples.

And, as he had sometimes in the pursuit of this peculiar fad to break into those churches to climb up into the steeples, so he broke into Literature from the inside, and left his mark.

Noticing, even at fifteen, that most of the "Notes and Queries" in the *Boston Transcript* were requests for lost doggerels, he induced a boy friend to write to the editor and ask for the author of a poem—one of G. B.'s own private effusions. And the next week, he himself sent in, and proudly he saw printed his answering letter and poem.*

With this merry literary achievement he was for some years content; he made no further attempts to create a demand for his work. G. B. a civil engineer would be.

The Massachusetts Institute of Technology, where he became, in four years, a Bachelor of Science, had, no doubt, although indirectly, a strong influence upon his imagination. It gave him precision of thought, if not direction. It made his ideas definite. It did not, however, encourage the pursuit of letters, except perhaps the Alphas Betas and Deltas which nearly conquered him in Stresses and Strains and the Theory of Elasticity.

Alas, the fates denied the young poet's desire to build tunnels and bridges in the fastnesses of the Andes. He was too good a

---

*The poem referred to is "Hope's Stultitude," and is included in this collection, p. 97.

draughtsman to be sent into the field; and three years of office work in San Francisco (usually with a poem or sketch concealed under his maps) sickened him of science.

A call to the University of California as Instructor in Topographical Drawing soon gave him the opportunity and leisure to indulge his muse. But, ere three years of this unseemly dignity had passed, a midnight escapade, though it endeared him to the students, brought an intimation from the President that his resignation from the Faculty of the U. C. would be accepted.

It was this pulling down of the cast-iron statue of the famous Dr. Coggswell—so long an aesthetic scandal in San Francisco—that launched G. B. into a literary career. With Bruce Porter, another of the iconoclasts, he started *The Lark*. This was to be known, during its two years' sprightly existence, as the most original magazine ever published in America.

In its initial number one nonsense rhyme achieved for G. B. a fame which he has made a lifelong attempt to surpass. This was

> I never saw a Purple Cow,
> I never Hope to See one;
> But I can Tell you, Anyhow,
> I'd rather See than Be one!

The Lark was unique in that it contained neither satire, parody, nor comment or criticism of any kind upon contemporary writers. Every page, in fact, was a definite contribution of appealing originality. Nonsense, serious verse, essays, fiction, drawings, inventions—*The Lark* was versatile—all had the freshness and gayety of youth. Its creed was optimism and *joie de vivre*. And most of it was written by G. B.; often the whole number, from cover design to jocose advertisements, was from his pen.

As a nonsense writer, however, he was still best known and enjoyed; and these two poems came near to rivaling his P. Cow.

> The Window has four little Panes—
> But One have I.
> The Window Panes are in its Sash—
> I Wonder Why!
>
> The Towel hangs upon the Wall—
> And Somehow, I don't Care at All.

The Door is Open. I must Say
I rather Fancy it That Way!

Amongst the many gallimaufries in *The Lark* was an essay consisting of six paragraphs each of which could be used in combination with any other, haphazard, making an infinite number of apparently logical permutations.*

Equally erudite was a short, pointed story in the key of A-sharp, by G. B. which began—and continued quite as extravagantly— with this burst of verbiage:—all words guaranteed genuine:

An autumnal sun, hanging in abditative attitude behind the atramental abysses of the wood, peered through the apertures of the adustive foliage, casting ampliated, anfractuous penumbric anamorphoses of the arbuscles in the Park. In the arbor, beneath an acacia, sat the austere Anthea, analytical, yet attrehent.

and the following attempt of a typewriting machine at automatic poetry is a patent satire upon all machine-made verse:

> Oh Phliis, "j??zVbx Aj%5 2q part,
> So soon—ıQ'k"jyx,-, 2-morrow,
> Alas, qıQ)$ 'Vmlj-; my poor heart!
> Ah—$$,%, ws 4pdv7, Qkcd, sorrow.
>
> Fare"well,. . QJmdubz$ "-,never mind,
> Sweet Phylli$, "jzf%ı ,-missing—
> Ah me,, v$%Aw"mjx . . js$. .have to find
> Another g$irlx $993% to do $gzk kissing!

The Burgess Nonsense Book containing many of *The Lark's* best humorous features and other eccentricities coined by G. B.'s whimsical mind, put him in a class apart. There have been few volumes of sheer, premeditated absurdity—too few. For Wit and Humor are more common than is generally supposed. Parody and Burlesque, too, are easy enough. Satire we find in spots. But Nonsense is a ticklish medium to essay. It takes a clear head to walk that narrow steep pathway along the wall of Pomposity without falling into the abyss of Silliness.

A fatal facility with rhyme, when combined with some talent

---

* The reader who doesn't believe it can try for himself. The "Interchangeable Philosophical Paragraphs" are reprinted on pp. 78-79.

as a grotesque illustrator and that cursed sense of humor to boot, was a seductive trio—almost irresistible. Luckily G. B. was able to steer these three Graces in a didactic direction, and escape motley for a while. The invention of a queer new race of beings, ill-behaved children—he callēd them Goops (it was a quaint word, once)—started him as a nursery Mentor. Book after book of Goops inculcating principles of infant etiquette in verse, and illustrated by himself with eccentric drawings, have made him now even better known as a juvenile writer than as a nonsense poet.

Little need be said of G. B.'s more serious literary work—novels, plays, poems and essays. But one must take its existence into consideration in appraising his work as a humorist. For humor is a natural reflex from serious and earnest impulses. The first arboreal anthropoid ape who, safe at the top of his tree, cackled in primitive laughter at the sight of his fellow at the bottom being attacked by a deadly enemy, felt something of what we call humor. And it was because that ancestor of ours knew by experience the seriousness of the other's plight that he made primordial fun of him. It might be said, indeed, that not only are humorists the most sapient commentators upon life, but that no one who cannot be earnest can be really funny.

And especially is this true of that form of applied humor called satire, which is never successful unless the subject ridiculed is well understood, if not indeed beloved. G. B. is always like one who chaffs his brother or his best friend—or, so far as that goes, himself.

G. B.'s ever-youthful play instinct has always had a way of breaking out in the most unexpected and joyful directions. He has spent a fortnight constructing a completely equipped miniature farmhouse, with mica windows, and green velvet lawns—only to set it afire for the amusement of a dinner party. He has built dozens of Nonsense Machines—most elaborate assemblies of mechanisms, whose sole object was to be busy in the most complicated possible way without doing anything useful whatever. With T. R.'s he once set out on a trip abroad to buy a foreign title—and ended by digging up first century B.C. Roman tombs in Provence. He published in San Francisco, with another madcap, Porter Garnett, a magazine of rankest nonsense, *Le Petit*

Journal des Refusées, and printed every copy on a different pattern of wall paper. And he exhibited, in an exclusive gallery on Fifth Avenue, some thirty water colors ambitiously hight "Experiments in Symbolistic Psychology." With Will Irwin, too, he collaborated not only on two books, but also in the management of the San Francisco & Arcady Railroad, an 87-foot line laid all over the floor of Suicide Hall, the apartment they shared on East Twenty-third Street.

Now do not these enthusiastic avocations cast a brilliant side-light on G. B. as a writer? It will be seen in this psychoanalysis that his mind is essentially scientific, rather than dramatic. His permutative System of Philosophy, his employment of every known French form of verse in *The Lark,* his sarcastic comments on Art, even the mechanical accurate quality of his drawings—all exhibit the same ironic, accuracy-loving, but law-breaking mind. To overcome technical difficulties, and at the same time exploit a really satiric idea, is his delight.

It will be seen by this time that G. B. loves *tours-de-force.* He loves machinery, and the intricacies of technique. He loves the extravagant, the outrageous. But he uses his gift always to demonstrate the absurdities of life. He creates his characters only to destroy them. He formulates complex theories and blows them up with blasts of laughter. He is amused at everything, respects nothing. It is all he can do to be merely decorous.

In one of his water colors, symbolizing Fancy, G. B. showed a Liverbone (another of his whimsical creations) who has leaped from the roof of a castle, and is seated, horseback, atop the moon. That bizarre, outlandish, care-free creature might also represent G. B.'s own mind. Say, Gertie, wouldn't it be awful to be like that?

TABLE OF

C O N T E N T S

NOTE. — The Author desires to acknowledge the permission to reprint articles contained in this book, kindly offered by the editors of *Life, Truth, St. Nicholas,* the *Puritan,* the *Wave,* the *Sketch, Black and White, Madame,* and the *Century.*

This is THE MUSE OF NONSENSE:
   See!
Preposterously Strained is She;

Her Figures have nor Rule nor Joint
And so it's Hard to See the Point!

THE INVISIBLE BRIDGE: A Kind of Fable:
Please Understand it, if You're Able.

I'd Never Dare to Walk Across
A Bridge I Could Not See,

For Quite Afraid of Falling off
I Fear that I Should Be!

MY FEET: A Memoir, with a Phase
Resembling some Equestrian Ways.

My Feet they haul me Round the House,
They Hoist me up the Stairs;

I only have to Steer them, and
They Ride me Everywheres!

On CITY FLORA : — Semi-Culled
By One whose Fame is Somewhat Dulled.

There is a Theory Some Deny
That Lamp
Posts once were
Three Foot
High;

And a Little Boy
was Terrible Strong,
And he Stretched 'em out to 'Leven Foot
Long!

The Legend of THE GIANT HORSE:
'Tis quite Improbable, of Course.

Once there was a GIANT HORSE,
That Walked through all the Town,

A-Stepping into all the Roofs,
And Smashing Houses Down!

THE PURPLE COW'S Projected Feast:
Reflections on a Mythic Beast,
Who's quite Remarkable, at Least.

I NEVER SAW A PURPLE COW,

BUT I CAN TELL YOU, ANYHOW,

I NEVER HOPE TO SEE ONE;

I'D RATHER SEE THAN BE ONE!

On DIGITAL EXTREMITIES:
A Poem, and a Gem it Is!

I'd Rather have Fingers than Toes;

I'd Rather have Ears than a Nose;
And As for my Hair,
I'm Glad it's All There;

I'll be Awfully Sad, when it Goes!

The LAZY ROOF what Liked the Sun:
Or, How the Walls were Put Upon.

The Roof it has a Lazy Time
A-Lying in the Sun;

The Walls, they have to Hold Him Up;
They do Not Have Much Fun!

REMARKABLE ART: A Lesson Objective
In Animal Motion and Rules of Perspective.

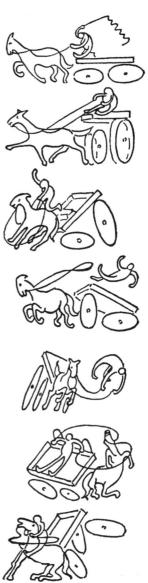

Remarkable
　　Truly is Art!
See — Elliptical
　　Wheels on a Cart!
It Looks Very Fair
In the Picture, up There,
But Imagine the
　　Ride, when you Start!

THE LECTURE: A Slight Divagation Concerning Cranial Ambulation.

I Love to Go to Lectures,
 And Make the People Stare,

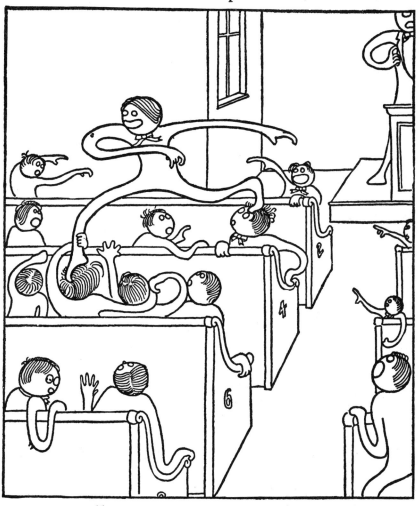

By Walking Round Upon Their Heads,
 And Spoiling People's Hair!

THE WINDOW PAIN: a Theme
    Symbolic,
Pertaining to the Melon Colic.

The Window has Four Little Panes;
But One have I —

The Window Pains are in its Sash;
I Wonder Why!

On STREETS OF GLUE : A Horrid
    Tale,
Of Fly-Paper on a Fearful Scale!

If the Streets were Filled with Glue,
What d' you S'pose that you would Do?

If you should Go to Walk, at Night,
In the Morning you'd be Stuck in Tight!

GLUE STREETS: A Picture Expurgated From out the *Lark* Because 't was Hated.

If the Streets were Filled with Glue,
What d' you S'pose that you would Do?

If you should Go to Walk, at Night,
In the Morning you'd be Stuck in Tight!

THE TOWEL AND THE DOOR, Ah, Well,
The Moral I'd not Dare to Tell!

The Towel Hangs Upon the Wall,
And Somehow, I don't Care, at All!

The Door is Open; I Must Say,
I Rather Fancy it That Way!

THE DOOR AND TOWEL, Once Again :
Preposterous, Inverse, Insane!

The Towel Hangs Upon the Wall,
And Somehow, I don't Care, at All!

The Door is Open; I Must Say,
I Rather Fancy it That Way!

INSOMNIA: Strange Membership,
And an Attachment Bound to Slip.

My Legs are so Weary
They Break Off in Bed;

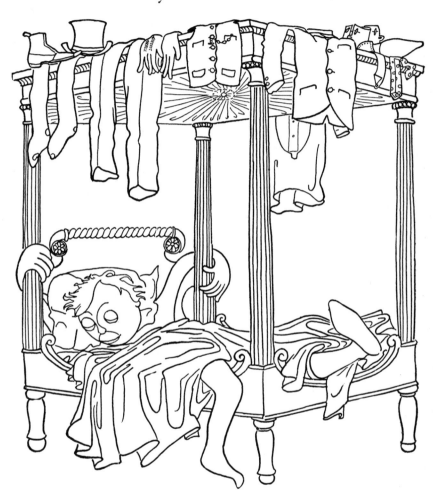

And my Caramel Pillow
It Sticks to my Head!

THE BORE: Or, How I am Impressed
By Coming of a Hateful Guest.

My House is Too Little to Live in;
Oh! What Would I do in a Flat?

With a Bore for a Caller
It Seems even Smaller;
There's Nothing so Strange about That!

PARISIAN NECTAR for the Gods:
A Little Thick, but What's the Odds?

Many People Seem to Think
Plaster o' Paris
Good to Drink;

Though Conducive unto Quiet,
I Prefer Another Diet!

THE FLOORLESS ROOM: A Novel Sort Of Argument Without Support.

I Wish that my Room had a Floor!
I don't so Much Care for a Door,

But this Crawling Around
Without Touching the Ground
Is Getting to be Quite a Bore!

ASTONISHMENT: Depicting How
Peculiar is the Verdant Bough!

I Picked Some Leaves from Off a Tree
And Then I Nearly Fainted;

For Somehow it Astonished Me
To Find They'd all been Painted!

A RADICAL CREED: Denying the Need
Of Things from Which we'd Dislike to be
Freed.

I Don't Give a $\sqrt{D^2}$
For the Stuff you Denominate Hair

And your Fingers and Toes and your
Neck and your Nose,
These are Things it Revolts me to Wear!

On DENSITY of a Remarkable Kind:
Usually Caused by an Absence of Mind.

If People's Heads were Not so Dense —
If We could Look Inside,

How clear would Show each Mood and
Tense —
How Often have I Tried!

THE GOOP: Constructed on a Plan
Beyond the Intellect of Man.

Now, You are what I call a GOOP

A
Co-Tangent,
Harmonious
Loop;

You Appear
to be Facing
Due South,

But Oh, What have you Done with your
Mouth?

THE SUNSET: Picturing the Glow
It Casts upon a Dish of Dough.

The Sun is Low, to Say the Least,
Although it is Well-Red;

Yet, Since it Rises in the Yeast,
It Should be Better Bred!

CONFESSION: and a Portrait, Too,
Upon a Background that I Rue!

Ah, Yes! I Wrote the "Purple Cow"—
I'm Sorry, now, I Wrote it!

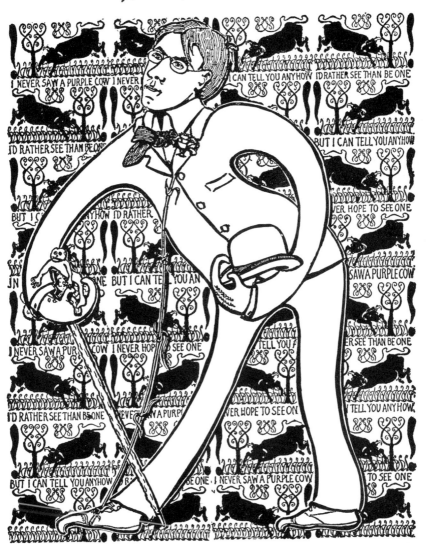

But I can Tell you Anyhow,
I'll Kill you if you Quote it!

MY HOUSE: and How I Make my Bed:
A Nocturne for a Sleepy Head.

My House is Made of Graham Bread,
Except the Ceiling's Made of White;

Of Angel Cake I Make my Bed—
I Eat my Pillow Every Night!

MY FANCIES: Fatuous Vagaries
Inspired by my Coal Hearted *Lares*.

My Fancies like the Flames Aspire;
I Dream of Fame and Fate;

I See my Future in the Fire,
And Oh, 't is Simply Grate!

THE PROPER EXIT: How a Jest
Politely Speeds the Parting Guest.

The Proper way to Leave a Room
Is not to Plunge it into Gloom;

Just Make a Joke Before you Go,
And Then Escape Before They Know.

THE JILTED FUNERAL: Motorcars More Deadlier than Mean Cigars!

Why does this Seedy Lady Look
As Though she Should be Undertook?

Ah, Should her Spirit now Forsake her,
I Wouldn't Want to Undertake her!

A QUADRUPED UNCLASSIFIED:
I couldn't Name This, if I Tried!

Now, Take this Gaudy Pseudo-Chair!
A Bold, Upholsterrific Blunder —

It doesn't Wonder Why it's There,
We don't Encourage it to Wonder!

THE BRITISH GUARDSMAN'S Well-
Packed Chest:
And Why his Martial Pride's Suppressed.

Who is this Man, so Tightly Dressed,
With Silver Medals on his Chest?

His Bosom does not Swell with Pride—
There is Not Room enough Inside!

On DRAWING–ROOM AMENITIES:
Oh, What a Happy Scene it Is!

There is Little in Afternoon Tea
To Appeal to a Person Like Me;

Polite Conversation Evokes the Elation
A Cow might Enjoy, in a Tree!

THE STAFF OF LIFE: And HOW
to Cut one;
Reproof, and How a Father Got One.

It Makes me (sic) and Mother Sick
To have you Cut the Bread so Thick;

I do not Care about your Waist,
It is a Question of Good Taste!

THE SENSE OF HUMOUR is Spontaneous,
Unconscious, — Instantaneous.

When you Get Off your Wheel,
Oh, how Funny you Feel!

When you Get Off your Joke
What a Gloom you Provoke!

On PREFERENCES one might Express
In Lingerie and Fitting Ad-dress.

I'd Rather have Callers than Cuffs,
Though Both of Them Render me Blue;

I'd Rather have Ribbons than Roughs,
But Why should that Interest you?

A WOMAN'S REASON: A Quotation
To Put an End to Conversation.

I'm Sure every Word that you say is
    Absurd;
  I Say it's all Gummidge and Twaddle;

You may Argue away till the 19th of May,
  But I don't like the Sound of the
    Moddle!

THE CALL: Effect of the Atrocity
Of Tales of Juvenile Precocity.

For an Hour they've been Saying "Good-
    Bye,"
And a Marvel of Patience am I;

I can Handle my Passion
Through Gossip and Fashion,
But at Mention of Babies I Fly!

THE POPLARS: How and Why they
Bowed;
A Delicacy Disavowed.

Perhaps you might Imagine that the Trees
Are Agitated Merely by the Breeze;

No, the Lady who so Fat is
Has been Eating Garlic Patties
And the Poplars are Afraid she's Going
to Sneeze!

WHAT SMITH TRIED TO BELIEVE: A Study That Ought to Appeal to Anybuddy.

WELL, I come home late that night, — near one o'clock, I reckon, and I undressed in the dark as per usual. When I got into bed, I thought it felt as though somebuddy had been there, and when I kicked out my leg, sure enough, somebuddy *was* there. Well, I thought, "Rats! What's the Difference? I'll go to sleep — it's only a man."

But I kinder could n't sleep, so I got up and lit a cigaroot, and I saw the feller what was in bed with me was dead. Well, I thought, "Rats! What's the Difference? He won't git over on to my side of the bed, anyway."

Well, I fired my cigaroot in the paper basket, and went to sleep. After a while, I thought I smelled smoke, and it was n't cigaroot smoke, neither, but the basket was all afire, and burning like a editor's soul after death! Well, I thought "Rats! What's the Difference?"

Well, it looked so bright and comfortable, I thought I'd get up and read. By this time one corner of the room was going like a runaway horse, and it was nice and warm. After I'd read about ten minutes, it got so blame hot I could n't stand it, and I got up and went into the next room. I just thought, " Rats! What's the Difference?"

Well, in about a hour, there was a big crowd outside of the old house, and they was all yelling " Fire!" to beat the cars. I looked outer winder. " Jump!" says a fireman, and I jamp.

Then I walked off, and a feller says, says he: " you blame fool, you bruk yer laig!" Well, I thought, " Rats! What's the Difference?"

A PERMUTATIVE SYSTEM: Oh, how Strange Philosophy's Kaleidoscopic Range!

IT may be doubted that any system of thought arranged upon the lines herewith proposed can be a success.

The fact of its accomplishment, alone, important as it must be, is no proof of method.

For instance, the correct relation between any two facts is one that must be investigated along the lines of thought best correlated to these facts.

And in spite of what, at first sight, might be called irrelevancy, there is this to be observed, no matter what bearing the above may have to the sub-

ject in hand, that the relation of one part to any other may or may not be true.

And here must be noted the importance of the demand that such types of thought do exist. This is, no doubt, a quality of subjects, rather than of relativity between modes of expression.

So, too, are questions affecting the expression of coherent symbols of equal importance with the methods by which these symbols are expressed.

But, at the same time, there must of necessity be a certain divergence in form between the types of questions to be discussed.

And in spite of what might, at first sight, be called irrelevancy, there is this to be observed, no matter what the above may have to the subject in hand, that the relation of one part to any other may or may not be true.

It may be doubted that any system of thought arranged upon the lines herewith proposed, can be a success. The fact of its accomplishment, alone, important as it must be, is no proof of method.

But, at the same time, there must of necessity be a certain divergence in form between the types of questions to be discussed.

For instance, the correct relation between any two facts is one that must be investigated along the lines of thought best correlated to these facts.

So, too, are questions affecting the expression of coherent symbols of equal importance with the methods by which these symbols are expressed.

And in spite of what, at first sight, might be called irrelevancy, there is this to be observed, no matter what bearing the above may have to the subject in hand, that the relation of one part to any other may or may not be true.

THE MEETING OF A SOCIAL CLUB:
at Which
(The Secretary's Minutes Seem to Show)
Proceedings did Not Go Without a Hitch.
If you have Ever Been to One, You'll Know!

SMITH

JONES   ROBINSON

*A*S *Mr. Smith still held the floor the chair objected to the
motion made by Mr. Jones as being out of order. . . .
Mr. Robinson, failing to receive his expected support,
and not being recognized by the chair, dropped out of the discussion,
there seemed to be a general desire to re-open the subject that had
been laid upon the table.*

THE "INSECT WORLD'S" Alarming Beat:
A Yellow Journalistic Feat.

OVER 1,000 DESTROYED IN KIT-CHEN!
REINFORCEMENTS TO GO TO THE FRONT!
GREAT HAVOC WITH SMOKELESS POWDER!

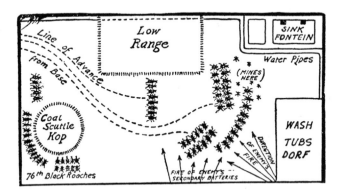

KIT-CHEN, July 31. — A dispatch exclusively to " The Insect World " brings the account of a horrible slaughter of more than 1,000 cockroaches in the neighborhood of Kit-Chen district. General Beetle, advancing toward Wash-Tubdorf was attacked with smokeless Buhach powder, and his whole command destroyed. The ground was covered with dead and dying and only a few of the wounded escaped to carry the news of the terrible calamity. The force was in the vicinity of an extensive Range, keeping in communication with the Water Pipes, near Sinkfontein, when the disaster occurred.

Reinforcements, now intrenched behind Coal-Scuttle-Kop, are about to advance into the Kit-Chen, led by General B. Tell of the Seventy-Sixth Black Roaches. The enemy is as yet invisible, but it is feared that another attack is imminent.

A SEMINARY FOR FEMALE SMOKING;—
A Needed Institution This. (No Joking!)

CURRICULUM:

FIRST YEAR: THE CIGARETTE.

Lighting. Plain Smoking. Knocking off Ash.
Inhalation. Smoking through Nose. The Nicotine Finger.
Laboratory Work: Rolling. Rice Papers and Corn Husks.

SECOND YEAR: THE CIGAR.

Sizes: Damas to Perfecto.
Colors: Claro to Maduro.
Stogies, Cheroots, and Seconds.
Laboratory Work: Fillers,
Binders and Wrappers.

THIRD YEAR: THE PIPE.

Filling and Packing.
Clays, Briars, and Meerschaums.
Water Pipes.
Laboratory Work : Coloring and
 Cleaning. Mixtures.
 Literature of Nicotine.

FOURTH YEAR: POST–GRADUATE COURSE.

Influence of Tobacco upon the Morals.
Smoke-Vortex-Rings.
The Peace-Pipe at Afternoon Tease.
Laboratory Work : Loaded Cigars and Gunpowder Pipes.
Use and Abuse of Holders. Street Practise.

MISS GULLIVER IN LILLIPUT:
Don't Say it is a Silly Cut —
I Did it with my Little Hatchet
You'll Find it Difficult to Match it !

MissGulliver

In Lilliput

THE LITTLE FATHER who Contracted
A Habit that a Loss Exacted.

THE elder Mr. Master was a big and bulky man
Before the queer event that I am telling you began;
His only son was Michael, then a little child of four,
But Michael has n't hardly any father any more!

It was little Michael Master, who detected, first of all,
That his great enormous father was becoming very small;
Now I never knew the reason, but I fancy that he shrank
Because of all the mucilage that Mr. Master drank.

Every day, at breakfast time, when Michael tried his dad,
He found he measured something less than yesterday he had;
And still he kept on growing small and smaller every night,
Till Michael and his father were exactly of a height!

There was no Mrs. Master, so the father and the son
Got on together happily and had a lot of fun;
They wore each other's clothing, and they used each other's
    toys,
They became as really intimate as if they both were boys!

But Mr. Master would persist in his eccentric drink,
So littler and littler did Mr. Master shrink.
They had to cut his trousers down; and soon they were afraid
They 'd have to send to Germany to have his Jaegers made.

The way he used up hats and shoes and linen shirts and ties!
As soon as they had bought them, he would need a smaller size!
But everywhere that Michael went, his father went, of course;
If Mr. Master could n't walk, he rode on Michael's horse.

The people used to laugh at him, when they went out to walk,
For Michael's tiny father made an awful lot of talk.
The little children in the street they always used to cry,
" *I* would n't have a father who was only two foot high ! "

But Michael was obedient to all his father told,
For though his daddy dwindled, he was forty-two years old!
And so when Michael misbehaved and tried to bite or scratch,
His father climbed upon a chair and beat him — with a match!

One day the Tax Collector called, and till he went away
The father hid in Michael's bank, because he could n't pay.
And when to burgle Michael's bank the Tax Collector tried,
" O, please don't shake the bank!" said Mike, " *my father is
inside!* "

One day a big policeman found him crying in the street,
" Oh, dear! I 've lost my father!" little Michael did repeat;
But ere the Bobby understood, he added with a smile,
" Oh, here he is! My dad was in my pocket all the while!"

And many other anecdotes do Michael's neighbors tell
Of this midget Mr. Master and his giant son as well;
Of how he swam in saucers and of how he hunted flies;
How proud he got to be about his Lilliputian size.

And Michael had to build a house to keep his father in,
A little paper house it was, the walls were very thin;
And if the child desired to have the morning to himself,
He put his father, with a lump of sugar, on the shelf.

He had to walk across the page and back, to read a book;
But he drank a drop of mucilage with every meal he took!
And when I last inquired about him, everybody said
That Michael used a microscope to put his pa to bed!

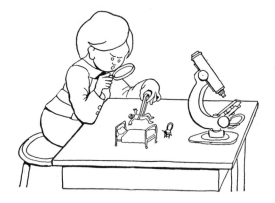

THE BOHEMIANS OF BOSTON and their Ways:
A Memory of the Jacobean Craze.

THE " Orchids " were as tough a crowd
As Boston anywhere allowed;
It was a club of wicked men —
The oldest, twelve, the youngest, ten;
They drank their soda colored green,

They talked of " Art " and " Philistine,"
They wore buff " wescoats " and their hair,
It used to make the waiters stare!
They were so shockingly behaved
And Boston thought them *so* depraved,

Policemen, stationed at the door,
Would raid them every hour or
     more!
They used to smoke (!) and laugh
     out loud (!)
They were a very devilish crowd!
They formed a Cult, far subtler,
     brainier,
Than ordinary Anglomania,
For all as Jacobites were reckoned,
And gayly toasted Charles the
     Second!
(What would the Bonnie Charlie
     say
If he could see that crowd to-day?)
Fitz-Willieboy McFlub-
     adub
          Was Regent of the Orchid's Club;

A wild Bohemian was he,
And spent his money fast and
     free.
He thought no more of spend-
     ing dimes
On some debauch of pickled
     limes,
Than you would think of
     spending nickels
To buy a pint of German
     pickles!
The Boston maiden passed
     him by

With sidelong glances of her eye,
She dared not speak (he *was* so wild),
Yet worshipped this Lotharian child.
Fitz-Willieboy was so *blasé*,
He burned a *Transcript* up, one day!
The Orchids fash-
ioned all their
style
On Flubadub's
infernal guile.
That awful Boston
oath was his, —
He used to jac-
ulate, "Gee-
Whiz!"
He showed them
that immoral
haunt,
The dirty Chinese
Restaurant,
And there they'd
find him, even when
It got to be as late as ten!
He ate chopped *suey* (with a fork),
You should have heard the villain talk
Of one *reporter* that he knew (!)
An artist, and an actor, too!!!
The orchids went from bad to worse,
Made epigrams — attempted verse!
Boston was horrified and shocked
To hear the way these Orchids mocked,

For they made fun of Boston ways,
And called good men Provincial Jays!
The end must come to such a story,
Gone is the wicked Orchids' glory,
The room was raided by police,
One night, for breaches of the Peace
(There had been laughter, long and loud,
In Boston this is not allowed),
And there, the sergeant of the squad
Found awful evidence, — my God! —
Fitz-Willieboy McFlubadub,
The Regent of the Orchids' Club,
Had written on the window sill,
This shocking outrage — " *Beacon H — ll!* "

THE KING SHALL COME BY HIS OWN:

VIVE LA REZTORATIN

HURRAH FOR tHE WHITE RoSE

THE MUSEUM OF KISSES: Surely No One could Visit it Demurely.

THIS is the place I'd like to burglarize;
It is the Royal Museum of Kisses.
It has an Annual Show, and gives a Prize
To all the most deserving men and misses.

And ranged in various rows about the wall
Are kisses, all deserving great attention;
But in one room, the sweetest, best of all,
Are those of one whose name I dare not mention!

ABSTROSOPHY: by which is Meant
A Theme of Nonsendental Bent.

I F echoes from the fitful past
  Could rise to mental view,
  Would all their fancied radiance last
Or would some odours from the blast,
 Untouched by Time, accrue?

Is present pain a future bliss,
 Or is it something worse?
For instance, take a case like this:
Is fancied kick a real kiss,
 Or rather the reverse?

Is plentitude of passion palled
 By poverty of scorn?
Does Fiction mend where Fact has mauled?
Has Death its wisest victims called
 When idiots are born?

HOPE'S STULTITUDE:
A Cheerful Lay;
At Least, *I* Like it, Anyway!

THE dismal day with dreary pace hath dragged its tortuous length along the grave-stones black and funeral vase cast horrid shadows long.

Oh let me die and never mourn upon the joys of long ago with cankering thoughts the world's forlorn — a wilderness of woe!

For in the grave's dark bed to be though grim and dismal it appears is sadder not it seems to me than harrowing nights of tears!

THE KNAVE OF HEARTS: If Euchred, List To my Advice, t' would Help you.   Whist!

THIS is the Knave of Hearts, beware!
Oh, trusting maidens, have a care!
There's not a Trick he will not do
To capture such a one as you!

Full many a Queen he's
made to blush,
For he enjoys a Royal
Flush.
But he will Bluff, and
he'll revoke her.
He is a most capricious
Joker.
For Jack is nimble, Jack
is cute —
Be careful how you Fol-
low Suit!
Trump though he is,
please understand,
You must not let him
Hold your Hand.
Oh, trust him not, until
the hour
You're certain he is
your Right Bower!

Then do not Cut him — let him Lead ;
He'll give you a good Deal, indeed !

THE PURPIL COWE: Perilla *Says* she Wrote it.
The Last Four lines are Mine, and So I Quote it.

A MAYDE there was, femely and meke enow,
    She fate a-milken of a purpil Cowe:
    Rofy hire Cheke as in the Month of Maye,
And fikerly her merry Songe was gay
As of the Larke vprift, wafhen in Dewe;
Like Shene of Sterres, fperkled hire Eyen two.
Now came ther by that Way a hendy Knight
The Mayde efpien in morwening Light.
A faire Person he was — of Corage trewe
With lufty Berd and Chekes of rody Hewe:
Dere Ladye (quod he) far and wide I 've ftraied
Vncouthe Aventure in ftraunge Contrie made
Fro Berwicke unto Ware.   Pardé I vowe
Erewhiles I never faw a purpil Cowe!
Fayn wold I knowe how Catel thus can be?
Tel me I pray you, of yore Courtefie!
The Mayde hire Milken ftent — Goode Sir she faide,
The Master's Mandement on vs ylaid
Decrees that in thefe yclept gilden Houres
Hys Kyne shall ete of nought but Vylet Floures!

AN ALPHABET OF FAMOUS GOOPS.

Which you'll Regard with Yells and Whoops.

Futile Acumen!

For you Yourselves are Doubtless Dupes

Of Failings Such as Mar these Groups —

We all are Human!

ABEDNEGO was Meek and Mild; he Softly Spoke, he Sweetly Smiled.
He never Called his Playmates Names, and he was Good in Running Games;
But he was Often in Disgrace because he had a Dirty Face!

BOHUNKUS would Take Off his Hat, and Bow and Smile, and
Things like That.

His Face and Hair were Always Neat, and when he Played he
did not Cheat;

*But Oh! what Awful Words he Said, when it was Time to Go
to Bed!*

The Gentle CEPHAS tried his Best to Please his Friends with
Merry Jest;

He tried to Help Them, when he Could, for CEPHAS, he was
Very Good;

*And Yet — They Say he Used to Cry, and Once or Twice he Told
a Lie!*

Daniel and Dago were a Pair who Acted Kindly Every-
where ;
They studied Hard, as Good as Gold, they Always did as
They were Told ;
They Never Put on Silly Airs, *but They Took Things that were
Not Theirs.*

Ezekiel, so his Parents said, just Simply *Loved* to Go to
Bed ;
He was as Quiet as could Be whenever there were Folks to
Tea ;
*And yet, he had a Little Way of Grumbling, when he should
Obey.*

When FESTUS was but Four Years Old his Parents Seldom
  had to Scold;
They never Called him "FESTUS DON'T!" he Never Whined
  and said "*I Won't!*"
*Yet it was Sad to See him Dine. His Table Manners were Not
  Fine.*

GAMALIEL took Peculiar Pride in Making Others Satisfied.
One Time I asked him for his Head. "*Why, Certainly!*"
  GAMALIEL Said.
He was Too Generous, in Fact. *But Bravery he Wholly
  Lacked.*

HAZAEL was (at Least he *Said* he Was) Exceedingly Well
Bred;
Forbidden Sweets he would not Touch, though he might Want
them very Much.
But Oh, Imagination Fails to quite Describe his Finger Nails!

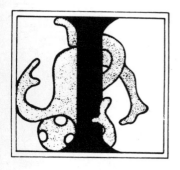 

How Interesting ISAAC Seemed! He never Fibbed, he Sel-
dom Screamed;
His Company was Quite a Treat to all the Children on the
Street;
*But Nurse has Told me of his Wrath when he was Made to Take
a Bath!*

Oh, Think of JONAH when you 're Bad; Think what a
Happy Way he had
Of Saying " *Thank You !* " — " *If you Please* " — " *Excuse
Me, Sir,*" and Words like These.
*Still, he was Human, like Us All. His Muddy Footprints
Tracked the Hall.*

Just fancy KADESH for a Name! Yet he was Clever All the
Same;
He knew Arithmetic, at Four, as Well as Boys of Nine or
More!
*But I Prefer far Duller Boys, who do Not Make such Awful
Noise!*

Oh, Laugh at LABAN, if you Will, but he was Brave when he
was Ill.

When he was Ill, he was so Brave he Swallowed All his
Mother Gave!

*But Somehow, She could never Tell why he was Worse when he
was Well!*

 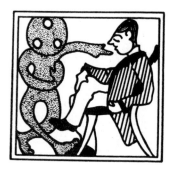

If MICAH's Mother Told him " *No* " he Made but Little of
his Woe;

He Always Answered, " *Yes, I'll Try!* " for MICAH Thought
it Wrong to Cry.

*Yet he was Always Asking Questions and Making quite Ill-timed
Suggestions.*

I Fancy Nicodemus Knew as Much as I, or even You;
He was Too Careful, I am Sure, to Scratch or Soil the
Furniture;
He never Squirmed, he never Squalled; *he Never Came when
he was Called!*

Some think that Obadiah's Charm was that he Never Tried
to Harm
Dumb Animals in any Way, though Some are Cruel when
they Play.
*But though he was so Sweet and Kind, his Mother found him
Slow to Mind.*

When PELEG had a Penny Earned, to Share it with his Friends
    he Yearned.

And if he Bought a Juicy Fig, his Sister's Half was Very Big!

Had he not Hated to Forgive, he would have been Too Good to
    Live!

When QUARTO's brother QUARTO Hit, was QUARTO Angry?
    Not a Bit!

He Called the Blow a Little Joke, and so Affectionately Spoke,

That Everybody Loved the Lad. *Yet Oh, What Selfish Ways*
    he Had!

Was Reuben Happy? I should Say! He laughed and Sang
the Livelong Day.

He Made his Mother Smile with Joy to See her Sunny-
Tempered Boy.

However, she was Not so Gay when Reub *Refused to Stop his
Play!*

When Shadrach Cared to be Polite, they Called him Gentle-
manly, Quite;

His Manners were Correct and Nice; he Never Asked for
Jelly Twice!

Still, when he Tried to Misbehave, O, how Much Trouble Shadrach *Gave!*

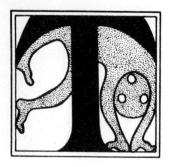

Don't Think that TIMOTHY was Ill because he Sometimes
  Kept so Still.
He knew his Mother Did Not Care to Hear him Talking
  Everywhere.
He did not Tease, he did Not Cry, *but he was Always Asking*
  "WHY?"

URIAH Never Licked his Knife, nor Sucked his Fingers, in
  his Life.
He Never Reached, to Help Himself, the Sugar Bowl upon
  the Shelf.
He Never Popped his Cherry Pits; *but he had Horrid Sulky
  Fits!*

To See young VIVIUS at his Work, you Knew he'd Never
Try to Shirk.

The Most Unpleasant Things he'd Do, if but his Mother
Asked him To.

*But when young Vivius Grew Big, it Seems he was a Norful
Prig!*

Why WABAN always Seemed so Sweet, was that he Kept so
Clean and Neat.

He never Smooched his Face with Coal, his Picture Books
were Fresh and Whole.

He washed His Hands Ten Times a Day; *but, Oh, what
Horrid Words he'd Say!*

What shall I say of XENOGOR, Save that he Always Shut the
Door !

He always Put his Toys Away when he had Finished with his
Play.

*But here his List of Virtues Ends. A Tattle-Tale does not Make
Friends.*

YERO was Noted for the Way with which he Helped his
Comrades Play ;

He 'd Lend his Cart, he 'd Lend his Ball, his Marbles, and
his Tops and All !

*And Yet (I Doubt if you' ll Believe), he Wiped his Nose upon his
Sleeve !*

The Zealous ZIBEON was Such as Casual Callers Flatter Much.

His Maiden Aunts would Say, with Glee, " How Good, how Pure, how Dear is He ! "

And Yet, he Drove his Mother Crazy — he was so Slow, he was so Lazy !

F I N I S

SO ENDS THE TOME: ARE YOU, MY FRIEND,
AS GLAD AS I TO SEE THE END?
HAVE YOU DONNED MOTLEY FOR THE MONEY
AND FEARED YOUR JESTS WERE NONE TOO FUNNY?
SO ENDS THE TOME: SO ENDS MY FOLLY;
'TIS DISMAL WORK, THIS BEING JOLLY.
NO MORE I'LL PLAY THE HARLEQUIN
UNLESS MORE ROYALTIES COME IN.